2020

THE YEAR WITHOUT WISDOM

Elder Bobby Morgan Sr.

2020 the Year Without Wisdom

By Elder Bobby Morgan Sr.

Designed by: Jazzy Kitty Publications

Cover created: Jazzy Kitty Publications

Logo designs: Andre M. Saunders/Jess Zimmerman

Editor: Anelda Attaway

Co-editor: Elder Bobby Morgan Sr.

© 2021 Bobby Morgan Sr.

ISBN: 978-1-954425-21-7

All rights reserved. This book is protected by the copyright laws of the United States of America. This book may not be copied or reprinted for commercial gain or profit. The use of short quotations or occasional page copying for personal or group study is permitted and encouraged. Permission will be granted upon request. Some actual scripture was used. For Worldwide Distribution, available in Paperback and eBook. Printed in the United States of America. Published by Jazzy Kitty Publishing, utilizing Microsoft Publishing Software.

ACKNOWLEDGMENTS

A special thank you to my parents for the foundation and stability given to me even as an adult.

Thank you to my beautiful children and my grandchildren, who always give me love and encouragement.

Thank you to the Mount Gilead Baptist Church. A congregation that truly gave me a home.

Thank you, God for Your Darling Son Jesus.

DEDICATION

This book is dedicated to the millions of Christians who in the face of such a trying year held to their Christian values morals and faith. That held fast in a year when true Christians were persecuted and attacked openly by so many others who wore the Evangelical banner but turned away from the duty and responsibility of an Evangelical life. Thank you for towing the line when so many others laid it down.

TABLE OF CONTENTS

INTRODUCTION..i
PART 1 - The Noticing..01
PART 2 – Tribulation...21
ABOUT THE AUTHOR......................................28

INTRODUCTION

This is a book from the viewpoint of a rational Christian. It gives insight to the normalcies of what rational thinking should be and decisions that should be made. By measuring them against all of the obviously wrong decisions and choices made by those connected with the former administration.

It is an account through the eyes of normal people with a measure of common sense and a measure of wisdom to place their faith in God and not man. It highlights the knowledge of mankind and how they lean more to their own knowledge and not God's wisdom, leading to hurt, pain, and the breakdown of society.

It also highlights the resiliency of a Christian faith displayed by a country standing strong and making right a bad decision made four years prior, proving that God is still in control.

PART 1

The Noticing

Wisdom is a weapon, it is as powerful as any bomb, gun, or army. Wisdom is foundationally the practical application of knowledge. Knowledge gives you information. Wisdom directs you how to and when to use that information.

Wisdom teaches you how to process. Wisdom teaches you when to speak and when to be silent. It teaches you when to fight and when to stand down.

Wisdom will always recognize authority. Authority is the pinnacle of God's word. Everything in creation was created by His word but upheld by His authority. All the acts of love performed in the Bible are upheld by God's authority. Every relationship under the sun will have relationship issues. However, all of them can be settled by recognizing God's authority and the one who God has placed that authority in concerning that relationship. Spiritual warfare is a necessity if wisdom is going to be effective. Spiritual warfare is overlooked because logic and desire are embraced. A self-agenda is a deterrent from performing God's will. Wisdom will always direct us away from selfish desires and towards God's will.

Isaiah 40:8 the grass Withers the flower fades but the word of our God shall stand forever.

Those words should mean something; however, there was the year 2020, the year wisdom was under attack. Leaders wouldn't lead, thieves ran the government, the judicial system opposed doing right by society, there were murders on prime-time television, and people supposedly of faith embraced the embodiment of racism, prostitution, thievery, extortion, abuse of power, murder, and so many other immoral infractions. There were mass shootings that took lives. There were misuses of power that took lives. There was a government that turned its back on the people they were supposed to represent and that took lives. There was a president that saw the world as his personal kingdom and that took lives.

Then there was Covid-19, a virus that would ravage the world and change life as we know it. However, the disease itself would need help to reach its full potential. It was received by its greatest ally in the form of President Donald J. Trump. He lied, he stole, he bullied, he enabled, and he abandoned all wisdom.

The year 2020 hosted several people with a wealth of knowledge and very smart but lacked godly wisdom. Our money says In God We Trust. Our Pledge of Allegiance says we are one nation under God; however, at every turn, God was being challenged. Being smart gives you a false sense of superiority, but wisdom gives you a solid foundation and access to unlimited favor and power through our Lord and Savior, Jesus Christ. The leaders of government had replaced wisdom, thus replacing God with selfish personal agendas. The lack of wisdom caused those in power to be narcissistic, condescending, mean, and without empathy, compassion or morality.

The country was nearly completely left to fend for itself because of the lack of leadership. Families were hopeless, jobless, homeless, and helpless but not broken. Unlike those we had chosen to represent us through legislation, there were many who would band together. Not as Blacks or Whites or any other color or nationality but as people. They fed each other, they comforted one another, and they stood up for one another. Their actions were the blueprint for what our leaders should have been doing. But it was 2020 and all governing wisdom had left the government.

Society is in turmoil, fear, anger, and rebellion have the nation in an unrelenting grip causing it to be in a downward spiral.

There is fear of the Covid-19 pandemic. There is fear of mounting judicial injustice. There is fear of the lack of leadership coming from Washington and the total absence of leadership coming from the president and the White House. But in all of this, there is hope. Even one loss of life due to Covid-19 is too many, but there are stories of triumph. Many people have found their way back to God because of the steps that have been required because of it. Sometimes God has to interrupt our daily lives to remind us who we are and of our godly duties. The pandemic had to come first because so many of us were living and working past the injustice that has always been here. For the last several years, it has become so embolden that it didn't even fear public ridicule.

While we do not want to champion a pandemic, we as Christians should be able to see that God took something bad and pulled something out of it that was good. We were forced into staying home, so we had time. We were glued to the television, so we were informed. But while being informed about this saddening loss of life because of the pandemic, we also saw the loss of life because of injustice. Then there was anger.

Then came rebellion (rightfully so) against what can only be described as modern-day tyranny. Now there's absolute defiance because of the leadership that seems to want to be served by the people rather than being of service to the people. Jesus was a servant, He used all of His Heavenly attributes to serve people. To enrich and fulfill their lives, to bring comfort and peace to them even if it caused discomfort to Himself.

He never sought to be a dictator. He never

challenged the will of His Father and He never threw anyone away. The model that Washington is governing by is broken. I encourage them to look at the Life of Christ because it is a portrait of how to treat the people.

The Bible tells of an incident where the disciples are caught in a storm, and it seems as if they are all going to perish on the sea. But suddenly, the one they had chosen (Jesus) comes to their rescue walking on the water and no one is lost. The ones we had chosen did not show up in our storm.

The ones we elected to be there for us didn't come to the rescue. While their wealth grew, so did the suffering of their constituents. Police officers became vigilantes. The media, in many cases, became judge and jury, and the refusal of indictment became their shelter. But even then, it did not extinguish the hope of the people. While the media had become judge and jury, there were those in the media that chose to fight. They chose to stand against those in their own field because their morality had not been corrupted, but their inner warrior had been awakened. They held on to the righteousness of accountability and traveled only in the lanes of truth.

The viciousness of the year 2020 would challenge them, but they would not back down. Satan used the media to oppress, but God had intervened to use it to strengthen and inspire. True Christians begin to pray harder and seek God more fervently and pray for those in media outlets who God had begun to use as champions for His people.

Satan is the original sinner. He was created as an archangel, a light bearer, perfect in beauty, strength, and wisdom. At some point, he despises his position. He wants to be recognized as God himself. The president in the year 2020 had many of the same attributes. He did not apologize for anything because in his own eyes, he did no wrong.

He operated outside of all designed laws. He broke all of the rules that his predecessors followed. He withheld information that would have saved us and gave information that would kill us. The wisdom of truth did not just elude him, it was his sworn enemy, and he sought to destroy it. Jesus called Satan a liar and the father of lies, in whom there is no truth, and that he was a murderer from the beginning. The 45th president of the United States can be described no differently.

Wisdom is the foundation upon which the future is built and in its absence, the future was in danger. People were afraid, hurt, and dying.

Allies of old did not trust us. Countries around the world lost respect for us. The once global leader, because of one man's hatred and ignorance, became weak and unwanted on the world stage. Without wisdom, there can be no prosperity that will last.

A third of the Bible is on how to live in the present and treat others. Jesus not only promised to come again, but He also promised to build His church and that the gates of Hell would not prevail against it. He built that church through the Holy Spirit and the believers who followed Him by faith and with wisdom.

A senate that in partiality knew no truth, a senate that had no character, and a senate without integrity. Ninety-nine percent of the Senate Republicans not only fell in line with the president, but they also enabled him. They embraced his decisiveness and evil. They coward beneath name-calling and public ridicule. They sold out friends and turned their backs on families in need as well as their sacred oath to preserve and protect the constitution. All wisdom was gone. But God still remains. He tells us He would never leave us nor forsake us and He never has. We the people were ridiculed, ostracized, taking advantage of, and in many instances left to die, but God always showed up and stepped in with Love and Power. It seemed as if those in power wanted those in need to perish; however, God wanted us to live.

2020 is the year wisdom left, but it is also the year strength was found in a Democratic party; there were those that began to show strength and stand against a female Democratic leader whose pride would blind her to the needs of the people. Without knowing, she became a part of the machine that ravaged and starved the people while holding the power to help them.

But the people persevered. Those around her begged her to compromise, but their pleas fell on deaf ears, but the people persevered. She would choose nothing over something; she would choose hate over love. Her distain for the president and his corrupt party would outgrow her will to help, helpless people and the result is that families suffered. The wisdom that she started with was overtaken by the anger she lived with and without wisdom, there is no clear path to victory.

The lack of wisdom left 2020 dry and barren but not broken. Though the people were hurting, their spirits were strengthened it, however, would come a time when a greater challenge would arise. The Bible says the latter will be greater than the former.

As a society, we should have been getting stronger, smarter, and wiser. Unfortunately, as our knowledge grew, so did our anger, rebellion, maliciousness, lack of decency, and respect. All of these things can be attributed to the lack of wisdom. Wisdom can halt the wheels of anger. Wisdom can give you the strength to endure the deepest pit. Wisdom comes from a relationship with Christ. For a wise man knows in and with Christ, he can do anything and without Him he is nothing.

During the '90s, a change occurred in the C.F.R. and other one-world advocates. They became more visible and open about their intentions. The war in the gulf provided an example of what could be done through world unity when a dictator like Saddam Hussein flexed his muscles. The master planners could not permit him to continue his grab for the world's oil, so in the name of the United Nations, the U.S. military put on one of its last demonstrations of power until the war in Afghanistan. We would go on to have other conflicts. One idea suggested that a steppingstone to a world government might be to divide the world into 10 regions with a head appointed to lead each area with representation at the U.N. The security council could be expanded to 10; consequently, the world would be governed by what a major US newspaper described as the 10 wise men.

Fast forward to 2020, the president has for four years been leading the country basically unchecked by the systems and mechanisms put in place to govern the president. He has ignored the constitution, he's bullied the Senate, and because of the cowardness of a Republican Congress, he has basically shackled the powers of the House of Representatives. He is establishing a foothold to dictatorship.

Wisdom would tell us to stand on principle, but cowards are deaf. Wisdom would tell us to resist, but cowards choose to seek peace out of weakness and fear rather than show character and strength. The book of Ecclesiastes says, *(there is a time and season for everything)* this was clearly a time to stand. But only wise men will listen to God. Revelations 13 and second Thessalonians 2 clearly predict that the governments of the world will relinquish their sovereignty to one head, an international world leader. However, few Christians are ever found in such groups. Wisdom is also a barrier that keeps those who truly believe from being overtaken by pride, greed, and ignorance. Therefore, no true follower of Christ would blindly follow anyone else.

The year 2020 was one of the most challenging in recent history because our leaders lacked the compassion, decency, and respect of their predecessors. People need to be loved as well as share their love with others. The year

2020 saw a tremendous divide; people were challenged in their faith and challenged in the day-to-day lives. Racism once again was being displayed in a manner that had long been kept in check. Always present but dealt with in a manner that was judicially tolerable. Hate began to spread throughout the country. Even spiritual advisors were choosing sides; the problem is it was not the side of Christ. Love conquers all, but in its absence, hate reigns supreme. The wisdom to show camaraderie and compassion had been muzzled. Hatred ruled the White House. Contempt ruled the Senate and stubbornness openly ruled the House of Representatives. The outcome is that the country suffered. Jesus our Lord and Savior, is the only one who can give salvation which can only come by personal faith in Him, never by works of righteousness.

The country needed help, and our leaders gave very little. The country needed healing, but the pandemic was fighting to keep that from happening. However, what the country needed most was saving.

The country needed salvation; the country needed Jesus, not an abundance of good works out of necessity, but true acts of righteousness out of love through Christ. While the country needed a spiritual awakening, the president was busy trying to establish himself as a dictator and further damaging the country. The president would have surprising help coming from White evangelicals who would turn a blind eye and a deaf ear to the will of God, giving their total allegiance to the president, thus giving him the loyalty that should only belong to God. They had replaced the deity of God with their own version chosen by ballot. The idea that they could embrace an evil man's ways and give him the label of being Christian and think God would bless it is borderline blasphemy. Whether it be Gaia, Buddha, Muhammad, or Trump, they are not in the same category as Christ.

The Bible is clear that the only way to the Father is through the Son, which is Jesus Christ our Lord. The year 2020 was also an election year. A year in which we would have the opportunity to write the wrongs we faced the last four years by choosing the leader that had been chosen for our country. This time wisdom would prevail.

We the people in an overwhelming majority would choose character, integrity, professionalism, and respect in the form of a new president and regime that dared to stand and say no more. Wisdom was making a comeback.

It would be challenged vigorously by allegations of fraud, by the president's denials of defeat and attempts of sabotage. He would refuse the peaceful transfer of power. He would contest the election in court, rile up half of the country, and in turn hold the nation hostage, but wisdom would prevail. Isaac Asimov said one of the saddest aspects of life right now is that science gathers knowledge faster than society gathers wisdom. Society had made a wise choice. It had chosen to turn away from hate and political bias and, in doing so, given wisdom an opportunity to return.

Even in politics, wisdom is to follow the examples of Christ. There is no question as to where Christians should stand in the political spectrum.

The Bible is clear that if you are a follower of Christ, you are a supporter of seeing the sick be healed; that means having healthcare. It means you can't be okay with hundreds of thousands dying when you have the means to help them. It means feeding the hungry, welcoming your neighbor. It means you can't be against programs that would help the poor. The door had been opened, and wisdom began to surge. The country was proving that while we are a nation of laws, there was still a measure of strength that lied in our morals which are founded in and on our faith.

PART 2

Tribulation

One of the worst attributes connected to the tribulation is the various plagues that will strike the entire existence of humankind. Those who turn their backs on what it truly means to be a Christian rejects the Savior and refuse to have their name written in the Lamb's Book of Life. The word "plague" appears eight times in the book of Revelations and is a part of the first birth pains mentioned by Jesus. Most of these plagues are the results of man's inhumanity to man. Without wisdom to lead us, the plagues of the tribulation will be so seriously ravaging that only a small percent of the world's population will remain, notwithstanding the rapture. The wisdom that was surging represented hope, which had for so long been in short supply. One of the things that will come with the tribulation is the breaking of the seven seals. The first seal introduces what is considered to be the alpha of those known to be the four horsemen of the apocalypse.

He is said to have a bow; however, he carries no arrow. This symbolizes that he has military strength but will do most of his conquering through political diplomacy. The year 2020 saw domestic militias rise in service of the 45th president. Civilians walked the streets with military gear and assault rifles, ready at a moment's notice to break the law and abandoned peace and decency in service of their leader. Revelations 6:1-2 seemed as if it were happening before our very eyes. Revelation 6:5-6 tells us the third horseman of the apocalypse, who early in the tribulation will take a heavy toll in deaths due to sickness. While we don't know what plagues the tribulation brings, we do know of cancer, heart disease, and diabetes.

Sexually transmitted diseases have grown and mutated to where former treatments have become ineffective. Then there are aids, sars, and then there came Covid-19. It seemed as if it could think; it maneuvered as if it had thought and guidance. The wisdom that we had abandoned had strengthened what we feared most. Our only hope was The surge of wisdom that was fighting to make its return. The surge of wisdom that the world was experiencing through Christ Jesus was our only hope.

I think human life is threatened as never before in modern history. I am one who believes it to be extremely hard to see how the human race is to combat its current state; evil always considers itself to be doing right.

At the rate humankind is consuming anger, it won't be long before the world is primed for another holocaust, which means that the return of Christ is imminent. The year 2020 should be a wake-up call to seek the wisdom of Christ and the guidance of Heaven. The political nightmare of 2020 was the breaking point for friendships, relationships, and even family. It also was the door in huge measure to opportunity for unmitigated violence and social destruction. The world health organization has determined that infectious diseases are the world's leading cause of death, killing 17 million people a year. This world has not seen the end of new epidemics. Primarily because of curiosity and man's God complex meaning the fascination to create and end life. Again this desire is due to a lack of wisdom. The plagues of the tribulation will scour the Earth as scripture says it will and only those wise enough to accept salvation will be spared by the rapture.

A story is told of a humble janitor of a small

town seminary who was waiting for the students to finish a basketball game so he could sweep the gym floor. While the janitor was waiting, he began to read his Bible. One of the students saw him and asked what he was reading? He replied Revelations. The young man didn't believe that a lowly janitor could understand the book of Revelations. He didn't believe anyone without the proper education could understand prophecy, especially a man who had not graduated from high school. The student asked the janitor if he understood what he was reading. The janitor, with a smile, replied, "Yes, it says we win."

2020 is almost a mirror or practice for those of us who believe. The chaos, the turmoil, the willingness of so many to turn to other gods. Who weren't sovereign but won the position through an election will be a choice that so many regret. Ones who cloaked themselves in biblical treason and misinformation. Wisdom does many things; one of the things it does which is widely overlooked, is give you strength. The leaders of 2020 were extremely vile and weak. But more importantly, they were weak because they were unwise. The lack of wisdom was the strength of their weakness. I'd rather have a janitor's wisdom rather than a politician's knowledge.

Maurice Switzer said, "It is better to remain silent at the risk of being thought a fool than to talk and remove all doubt of it."

Paulo Coelho said, "The secret of life, though, is to fall seven times and to get up eight times."

Though the enemy would scream and yell, the nation would get up. The weight that the country would have to shoulder would be tremendous, but we would get up. Four years of maliciousness hurt and pain, but through Jesus Christ our Lord, wisdom proved superior, and the nation stood up.

Believing in the light is never easy when surrounded by darkness. Hatred almost destroyed us, but love and wisdom through our Heavenly Father saved us. 2020 will be a year remembered for death, pain, and destruction. It will also be remembered as the year we took the enemies' best shot just like we always have, and when the dust settled, we were by the grace of God standing strong in victory.

ABOUT THE AUTHOR

Elder Bobby Morgan is the father of eight children, the current assistant pastor of the Mount Gilead Baptist Church of Gilmer, Texas. He is the former pastor of the Eastside Christian Church in Longview, Texas. He is also the founder and president of the United Christian fellowship. (U.C.F.) A non-profit ministry. Dedicated to doing the true work of Christ.

Contact Information

Email: mrgbob8@etex.net

Facebook: Mount Gilead Baptist

https://www.facebook.com/mount.g.church

www.ingramcontent.com/pod-product-compliance
Lightning Source LLC
LaVergne TN
LVHW020449080526
838202LV00055B/5395